2023 Monthly Planner with Budget Pages

I. S. Anderson

2023 Monthly Planner
with Budget Pages

Copyright © 2022 by I. S. Anderson

ISBN-10: 1-947399-39-X

ISBN-13: 978-1-947399-39-6

All rights reserved, including the right to reproduce this journal in whole or any portions thereof, in any form whatsoever.

For more information regarding this publication, contact: **nahjpress@outlook.com**

First Printing, 2022

2023 Monthly Planner
With Budget Pages

Belongs To:

_____

2023

JANUARY
S	M	T	W	T	F	S
1	2	3	4	5	6	7
8	9	10	11	12	13	14
15	16	17	18	19	20	21
22	23	24	25	26	27	28
29	30	31				

FEBRUARY
S	M	T	W	T	F	S
			1	2	3	4
5	6	7	8	9	10	11
12	13	14	15	16	17	18
19	20	21	22	23	24	25
26	27	28				

MARCH
S	M	T	W	T	F	S
			1	2	3	4
5	6	7	8	9	10	11
12	13	14	15	16	17	18
19	20	21	22	23	24	25
26	27	28	29	30	31	

APRIL
S	M	T	W	T	F	S
						1
2	3	4	5	6	7	8
9	10	11	12	13	14	15
16	17	18	19	20	21	22
23	24	25	26	27	28	29
30						

MAY
S	M	T	W	T	F	S
	1	2	3	4	5	6
7	8	9	10	11	12	13
14	15	16	17	18	19	20
21	22	23	24	25	26	27
28	29	30	31			

JUNE
S	M	T	W	T	F	S
				1	2	3
4	5	6	7	8	9	10
11	12	13	14	15	16	17
18	19	20	21	22	23	24
25	26	27	28	29	30	

JULY
S	M	T	W	T	F	S
						1
2	3	4	5	6	7	8
9	10	11	12	13	14	15
16	17	18	19	20	21	22
23	24	25	26	27	28	29
30	31					

AUGUST
S	M	T	W	T	F	S
		1	2	3	4	5
6	7	8	9	10	11	12
13	14	15	16	17	18	19
20	21	22	23	24	25	26
27	28	29	30	31		

SEPTEMBER
S	M	T	W	T	F	S
					1	2
3	4	5	6	7	8	9
10	11	12	13	14	15	16
17	18	19	20	21	22	23
24	25	26	27	28	29	30

OCTOBER
S	M	T	W	T	F	S
1	2	3	4	5	6	7
8	9	10	11	12	13	14
15	16	17	18	19	20	21
22	23	24	25	26	27	28
29	30	31				

NOVEMBER
S	M	T	W	T	F	S
			1	2	3	4
5	6	7	8	9	10	11
12	13	14	15	16	17	18
19	20	21	22	23	24	25
26	27	28	29	30		

DECEMBER
S	M	T	W	T	F	S
					1	2
3	4	5	6	7	8	9
10	11	12	13	14	15	16
17	18	19	20	21	22	23
24	25	26	27	28	29	30
31						

2024

JANUARY
S	M	T	W	T	F	S
	1	2	3	4	5	6
7	8	9	10	11	12	13
14	15	16	17	18	19	20
21	22	23	24	25	26	27
28	29	30	31			

FEBRUARY
S	M	T	W	T	F	S
				1	2	3
4	5	6	7	8	9	10
11	12	13	14	15	16	17
18	19	20	21	22	23	24
25	26	27	28	29		

MARCH
S	M	T	W	T	F	S
					1	2
3	4	5	6	7	8	9
10	11	12	13	14	15	16
17	18	19	20	21	22	23
24	25	26	27	28	29	30
31						

APRIL
S	M	T	W	T	F	S
	1	2	3	4	5	6
7	8	9	10	11	12	13
14	15	16	17	18	19	20
21	22	23	24	25	26	27
28	29	30				

MAY
S	M	T	W	T	F	S
			1	2	3	4
5	6	7	8	9	10	11
12	13	14	15	16	17	18
19	20	21	22	23	24	25
26	27	28	29	30	31	

JUNE
S	M	T	W	T	F	S
						1
2	3	4	5	6	7	8
9	10	11	12	13	14	15
16	17	18	19	20	21	22
23	24	25	26	27	28	29
30						

JULY
S	M	T	W	T	F	S
	1	2	3	4	5	6
7	8	9	10	11	12	13
14	15	16	17	18	19	20
21	22	23	24	25	26	27
28	29	30	31			

AUGUST
S	M	T	W	T	F	S
				1	2	3
4	5	6	7	8	9	10
11	12	13	14	15	16	17
18	19	20	21	22	23	24
25	26	27	28	29	30	31

SEPTEMBER
S	M	T	W	T	F	S
1	2	3	4	5	6	7
8	9	10	11	12	13	14
15	16	17	18	19	20	21
22	23	24	25	26	27	28
29	30					

OCTOBER
S	M	T	W	T	F	S
		1	2	3	4	5
6	7	8	9	10	11	12
13	14	15	16	17	18	19
20	21	22	23	24	25	26
27	28	29	30	31		

NOVEMBER
S	M	T	W	T	F	S
					1	2
3	4	5	6	7	8	9
10	11	12	13	14	15	16
17	18	19	20	21	22	23
24	25	26	27	28	29	30

DECEMBER
S	M	T	W	T	F	S
1	2	3	4	5	6	7
8	9	10	11	12	13	14
15	16	17	18	19	20	21
22	23	24	25	26	27	28
29	30	31				

Sample Budget Page

Income and Fixed Expenses

Month: *March*   Year: *2022*

Date	Source of Income	Amount
01/14	Salary	3,500.00
01/16	Rental income	1,800.00
01/21	Writing	900.00
01/28	Salary	3,500.00
	Total Income	9,700.00

Savings	Amount
Emergency fund	1,0000.00
Investments	2,000.00
Vacation	1,0000.00
Total Savings	4,000.00

Due Date	Fixed Expenses	Amount
01/02	Mortgage	2,200.00
01/07	Car insurance	150.00
01/10	Car payment	500.00
01/15	Internet	60.00
01/15	Subscriptions	40.00
	Total Fixed Expenses	2,950

Credit Card	Payment	Balance
Visa	300.00	0
Total	300.00	0

Total Income	9,700.00
- Total Fixed Expenses	2,950.00
- Total Credit Card Payment	300.00
- Total Savings	4000.00
Remaining Balance	2,450.00

Sample Budget Page

Weekly/Monthly Budget

Expense	Budgeted	Actual
Electricity	120.00	134.00
Water	70.00	70.00
Gas	170.00	165.00
Grocery	400.00	455.00
Personal care	200.00	150.00
Subtotal	960.00	974.00

Expense	Budgeted	Actual
Subtotal		

Subtotal		

Subtotal		

Summary	Amount
Previous Balance	2,450.00
- Total Actual Expenses	974.00
Remaining Balance	1,476.00

My Financial Goals

Goal:	Time Frame:
	Notes:

Goal:	Time Frame:
	Notes:

Goal:	Time Frame:
	Notes:

Goal:	Time Frame:
	Notes:

My Financial Goals

Goal:	Time Frame:
	Notes:

Goal:	Time Frame:
	Notes:

Goal:	Time Frame:
	Notes:

Goal:	Time Frame:
	Notes:

My Net Worth

Assets (What I Own)

Cash and Cash Equivalents	Amount
Checking account	
Savings account	
Money market account	
Cash value of life insurance	
Total	

Real Estate	Current Value
Principal home	
Vacation home	
Land	
Total	

Investments	Current Value
Certificates of deposit	
Stocks	
Bonds	
Mutual funds	
Annuity (accumulated value)	
IRAs	
401(k)/ 403(b) /457 plans	
Pension plan	
Total	

Personal Property	Current Value
Cars, trucks, boats	
Home furnishings	
Art, antiques, coins, collectibles	
Jewelry	
Total	
Total Assets	

Liabilities (What I Owe)

Current Debts	Amount Due
Credit card balances	
Estimated income tax owed	
Medical	
Legal	
Total	

Long-term Debts	Amount Due
Home mortgage	
Home equity loan	
Mortgage on rental properties	
Car loans	
Student loans	
Life insurance policy loans	
Total	
Total Liabilities	

Net Worth (Total Assets – Total Liabilities)	

Notes

My Net Worth

Assets (What I Own)

Cash and Cash Equivalents	Amount
Checking account	
Savings account	
Money market account	
Cash value of life insurance	
Total	

Real Estate	Current Value
Principal home	
Vacation home	
Land	
Total	

Investments	Current Value
Certificates of deposit	
Stocks	
Bonds	
Mutual funds	
Annuity (accumulated value)	
IRAs	
401(k)/ 403(b) /457 plans	
Pension plan	
Total	

Personal Property	Current Value
Cars, trucks, boats	
Home furnishings	
Art, antiques, coins, collectibles	
Jewelry	
Total	
Total Assets	

Liabilities (What I Owe)

Current Debts	Amount Due
Credit card balances	
Estimated income tax owed	
Medical	
Legal	
Total	

Long-term Debts	Amount Due
Home mortgage	
Home equity loan	
Mortgage on rental properties	
Car loans	
Student loans	
Life insurance policy loans	
Total	
Total Liabilities	

Net Worth	
(Total Assets – Total Liabilities)	

Notes

JANUARY 2023

SUNDAY	MONDAY	TUESDAY	WEDNESDAY
1 New Year's Day	2	3	4
8	9	10	11
15	16 Martin Luther King Jr. Day	17	18
22	23	24	25
29	30	31	

DECEMBER 2022
S	M	T	W	T	F	S
				1	2	3
4	5	6	7	8	9	10
11	12	13	14	15	16	17
18	19	20	21	22	23	24
25	26	27	28	29	30	31

JANUARY
S	M	T	W	T	F	S
1	2	3	4	5	6	7
8	9	10	11	12	13	14
15	16	17	18	19	20	21
22	23	24	25	26	27	28
29	30	31				

FEBRUARY
S	M	T	W	T	F	S
			1	2	3	4
5	6	7	8	9	10	11
12	13	14	15	16	17	18
19	20	21	22	23	24	25
26	27	28				

THURSDAY	FRIDAY	SATURDAY	NOTES
5	6	7	
12	13	14	
19	20	21	
26	27	28	
☐	☐	☐	
☐	☐	☐	
☐	☐	☐	
☐	☐	☐	
☐	☐	☐	

Income and Fixed Expenses

Month: _____   Year: _____

Date	Source of Income	Amount
	Total Income	

Savings	Amount
Total Savings	

Due Date	Fixed Expenses	Amount
	Total Fixed Expenses	

Credit Card	Payment	Balance
	Total	

Total Income		
-	Total Fixed Expenses	
-	Total Credit Card Payment	
-	Total Savings	
Remaining Balance		

Weekly/Monthly Budget

Expense	Budgeted	Actual
Subtotal		

Expense	Budgeted	Actual
Subtotal		

Subtotal		

Subtotal		

Summary	Amount
Previous Balance	
- Total Actual Expenses	
Remaining Balance	

Daily Expenses

Date	Description/Category	Amount		Date	Description/Category	Amount
		Total				Total

Daily Expenses

Date	Description/Category	Amount	Date	Description/Category	Amount
	Total			Total	

Ideas and Notes

Ideas and Notes

FEBRUARY 2023

SUNDAY	MONDAY	TUESDAY	WEDNESDAY
			1
5	6	7	8
12	13	14	15
19	20 **Presidents' Day**	21	22
26	27	28	

JANUARY
S	M	T	W	T	F	S
1	2	3	4	5	6	7
8	9	10	11	12	13	14
15	16	17	18	19	20	21
22	23	24	25	26	27	28
29	30	31				

FEBRUARY
S	M	T	W	T	F	S
			1	2	3	4
5	6	7	8	9	10	11
12	13	14	15	16	17	18
19	20	21	22	23	24	25
26	27	28				

MARCH
S	M	T	W	T	F	S
			1	2	3	4
5	6	7	8	9	10	11
12	13	14	15	16	17	18
19	20	21	22	23	24	25
26	27	28	29	30	31	

THURSDAY	FRIDAY	SATURDAY	NOTES
2	3	4	
9	10	11	
16	17	18	
23	24	25	
☐	☐	☐	
☐	☐	☐	
☐	☐	☐	
☐	☐	☐	
☐	☐	☐	

Income and Fixed Expenses

Month: _____   Year: _____

Date	Source of Income	Amount
	Total Income	

Savings	Amount
Total Savings	

Due Date	Fixed Expenses	Amount
	Total Fixed Expenses	

Credit Card	Payment	Balance
	Total	

Total Income	
- Total Fixed Expenses	
- Total Credit Card Payment	
- Total Savings	
Remaining Balance	

Weekly/Monthly Budget

Expense	Budgeted	Actual
Subtotal		

Expense	Budgeted	Actual
Subtotal		

Subtotal		

Subtotal		

Summary	Amount
Previous Balance	
- Total Actual Expenses	
Remaining Balance	

Daily Expenses

Date	Description/Category	Amount	Date	Description/Category	Amount
		Total			Total

Daily Expenses

Date	Description/Category	Amount		Date	Description/Category	Amount
		Total				Total

Ideas and Notes

Ideas and Notes

MARCH 2023

SUNDAY	MONDAY	TUESDAY	WEDNESDAY
			1
5	6	7	8
12	13	14	15
19	20	21	22
26	27	28	29

FEBRUARY
S	M	T	W	T	F	S
			1	2	3	4
5	6	7	8	9	10	11
12	13	14	15	16	17	18
19	20	21	22	23	24	25
26	27	28				

MARCH
S	M	T	W	T	F	S
			1	2	3	4
5	6	7	8	9	10	11
12	13	14	15	16	17	18
19	20	21	22	23	24	25
26	27	28	29	30	31	

APRIL
S	M	T	W	T	F	S
						1
2	3	4	5	6	7	8
9	10	11	12	13	14	15
16	17	18	19	20	21	22
23	24	25	26	27	28	29
30						

THURSDAY	FRIDAY	SATURDAY	NOTES
2	3	4	
9	10	11	
16	17	18	
23	24	25	
30	31		
☐	☐	☐	
☐	☐	☐	
☐	☐	☐	
☐	☐	☐	
☐	☐	☐	

Income and Fixed Expenses

Month: _____   Year: _____

Date	Source of Income	Amount
	Total Income	

Savings	Amount
Total Savings	

Due Date	Fixed Expenses	Amount
	Total Fixed Expenses	

Credit Card	Payment	Balance
	Total	

Total Income	
- Total Fixed Expenses	
- Total Credit Card Payment	
- Total Savings	
Remaining Balance	

Weekly/Monthly Budget

Expense	Budgeted	Actual
Subtotal		

Expense	Budgeted	Actual
Subtotal		

Subtotal		

Subtotal		

Summary	Amount
Previous Balance	
− Total Actual Expenses	
Remaining Balance	

Daily Expenses

Date	Description/Category	Amount
	Total	

Date	Description/Category	Amount
	Total	

Daily Expenses

Date	Description/Category	Amount	Date	Description/Category	Amount
	Total			Total	

Ideas and Notes

Ideas and Notes

APRIL 2023

SUNDAY	MONDAY	TUESDAY	WEDNESDAY
2	3	4	5
9	10	11	12
16	17	18	19
23	24	25	26
30			

MARCH
S	M	T	W	T	F	S
			1	2	3	4
5	6	7	8	9	10	11
12	13	14	15	16	17	18
19	20	21	22	23	24	25
26	27	28	29	30	31	

APRIL
S	M	T	W	T	F	S
						1
2	3	4	5	6	7	8
9	10	11	12	13	14	15
16	17	18	19	20	21	22
23	24	25	26	27	28	29
30						

MAY
S	M	T	W	T	F	S
	1	2	3	4	5	6
7	8	9	10	11	12	13
14	15	16	17	18	19	20
21	22	23	24	25	26	27
28	29	30	31			

THURSDAY	FRIDAY	SATURDAY	NOTES
		1	
6	7	8	
13	14	15	
20	21	22	
27	28	29	
☐	☐	☐	
☐	☐	☐	
☐	☐	☐	
☐	☐	☐	
☐	☐	☐	
THURSDAY	FRIDAY	SATURDAY	NOTES

Income and Fixed Expenses

Month: _____   Year: _____

Date	Source of Income	Amount
	Total Income	

Savings	Amount
Total Savings	

Due Date	Fixed Expenses	Amount
	Total Fixed Expenses	

Credit Card	Payment	Balance
	Total	

Total Income	
- Total Fixed Expenses	
- Total Credit Card Payment	
- Total Savings	
Remaining Balance	

Weekly/Monthly Budget

Expense	Budgeted	Actual
Subtotal		

Expense	Budgeted	Actual
Subtotal		

Subtotal		

Subtotal		

Summary	Amount
Previous Balance	
- Total Actual Expenses	
Remaining Balance	

Daily Expenses

Date	Description/Category	Amount		Date	Description/Category	Amount
		Total				Total

Daily Expenses

Date	Description/Category	Amount	Date	Description/Category	Amount
	Total			Total	

Ideas and Notes

Ideas and Notes

MAY 2023

SUNDAY	MONDAY	TUESDAY	WEDNESDAY
	1	2	3
7	8	9	10
14	15	16	17
21	22	23	24
28	29 Memorial Day	30	31

APRIL
S	M	T	W	T	F	S
						1
2	3	4	5	6	7	8
9	10	11	12	13	14	15
16	17	18	19	20	21	22
23	24	25	26	27	28	29
30						

MAY
S	M	T	W	T	F	S
	1	2	3	4	5	6
7	8	9	10	11	12	13
14	15	16	17	18	19	20
21	22	23	24	25	26	27
28	29	30	31			

JUNE
S	M	T	W	T	F	S
				1	2	3
4	5	6	7	8	9	10
11	12	13	14	15	16	17
18	19	20	21	22	23	24
25	26	27	28	29	30	

THURSDAY	FRIDAY	SATURDAY	NOTES
4	5	6	
11	12	13	
18	19	20	
25	26	27	
☐	☐	☐	
☐	☐	☐	
☐	☐	☐	
☐	☐	☐	
☐	☐	☐	

Income and Fixed Expenses

Month: _____   Year: _____

Date	Source of Income	Amount
	Total Income	

Savings	Amount
Total Savings	

Due Date	Fixed Expenses	Amount
	Total Fixed Expenses	

Credit Card	Payment	Balance
	Total	

Total Income		
-	Total Fixed Expenses	
-	Total Credit Card Payment	
-	Total Savings	
Remaining Balance		

Weekly/Monthly Budget

Expense	Budgeted	Actual
Subtotal		

Expense	Budgeted	Actual
Subtotal		

Subtotal		

Subtotal		

Summary	Amount
Previous Balance	
- Total Actual Expenses	
Remaining Balance	

Daily Expenses

Date	Description/Category	Amount
	Total	

Date	Description/Category	Amount
	Total	

Daily Expenses

Date	Description/Category	Amount	Date	Description/Category	Amount
	Total			Total	

Ideas and Notes

Ideas and Notes

JUNE 2023

SUNDAY	MONDAY	TUESDAY	WEDNESDAY
4	5	6	7
11	12	13	14
18	19	20	21
25	26	27	28

MAY
S	M	T	W	T	F	S
	1	2	3	4	5	6
7	8	9	10	11	12	13
14	15	16	17	18	19	20
21	22	23	24	25	26	27
28	29	30	31			

JUNE
S	M	T	W	T	F	S
				1	2	3
4	5	6	7	8	9	10
11	12	13	14	15	16	17
18	19	20	21	22	23	24
25	26	27	28	29	30	

JULY
S	M	T	W	T	F	S
						1
2	3	4	5	6	7	8
9	10	11	12	13	14	15
16	17	18	19	20	21	22
23	24	25	26	27	28	29
30	31					

THURSDAY	FRIDAY	SATURDAY	NOTES
1	2	3	
8	9	10	
15	16	17	
22	23	24	
29	30		
☐	☐	☐	
☐	☐	☐	
☐	☐	☐	
☐	☐	☐	
☐	☐	☐	

Income and Fixed Expenses

Month: _____   Year: _____

Date	Source of Income	Amount
	Total Income	

Savings	Amount
Total Savings	

Due Date	Fixed Expenses	Amount
	Total Fixed Expenses	

Credit Card	Payment	Balance
Total		

Total Income	
- Total Fixed Expenses	
- Total Credit Card Payment	
- Total Savings	
Remaining Balance	

Weekly/Monthly Budget

Expense	Budgeted	Actual
Subtotal		

Expense	Budgeted	Actual
Subtotal		

Subtotal		

Subtotal		

Summary	Amount
Previous Balance	
- Total Actual Expenses	
Remaining Balance	

Daily Expenses

Date	Description/Category	Amount
	Total	

Date	Description/Category	Amount
	Total	

Daily Expenses

Date	Description/Category	Amount	Date	Description/Category	Amount
	Total			Total	

Ideas and Notes

Ideas and Notes

JULY 2023

SUNDAY	MONDAY	TUESDAY	WEDNESDAY
2	3	4 Independence Day	5
9	10	11	12
16	17	18	19
23	24	25	26
30	31		

JUNE
S	M	T	W	T	F	S
				1	2	3
4	5	6	7	8	9	10
11	12	13	14	15	16	17
18	19	20	21	22	23	24
25	26	27	28	29	30	

JULY
S	M	T	W	T	F	S
						1
2	3	4	5	6	7	8
9	10	11	12	13	14	15
16	17	18	19	20	21	22
23	24	25	26	27	28	29
30	31					

THURSDAY	FRIDAY	SATURDAY	NOTES
		1	
6	7	8	
13	14	15	
20	21	22	
27	28	29	
☐	☐	☐	
☐	☐	☐	
☐	☐	☐	
☐	☐	☐	
☐	☐	☐	
THURSDAY	FRIDAY	SATURDAY	NOTES

Income and Fixed Expenses

Month: _____   Year: _____

Date	Source of Income	Amount
	Total Income	

Savings	Amount
Total Savings	

Due Date	Fixed Expenses	Amount
	Total Fixed Expenses	

Credit Card	Payment	Balance
	Total	

Total Income	
- Total Fixed Expenses	
- Total Credit Card Payment	
- Total Savings	
Remaining Balance	

Weekly/Monthly Budget

Expense	Budgeted	Actual
Subtotal		

Expense	Budgeted	Actual
Subtotal		

Expense	Budgeted	Actual
Subtotal		

Expense	Budgeted	Actual
Subtotal		

Summary	Amount
Previous Balance	
- Total Actual Expenses	
Remaining Balance	

Daily Expenses

Date	Description/Category	Amount
	Total	

Date	Description/Category	Amount
	Total	

Daily Expenses

Date	Description/Category	Amount	Date	Description/Category	Amount
		Total			Total

Ideas and Notes

Ideas and Notes

AUGUST 2023

SUNDAY	MONDAY	TUESDAY	WEDNESDAY
		1	2
6	7	8	9
13	14	15	16
20	21	22	23
27	28	29	30

JULY
S	M	T	W	T	F	S
						1
2	3	4	5	6	7	8
9	10	11	12	13	14	15
16	17	18	19	20	21	22
23	24	25	26	27	28	29
30	31					

AUGUST
S	M	T	W	T	F	S
		1	2	3	4	5
6	7	8	9	10	11	12
13	14	15	16	17	18	19
20	21	22	23	24	25	26
27	28	29	30	31		

SEPTEMBER
S	M	T	W	T	F	S
					1	2
3	4	5	6	7	8	9
10	11	12	13	14	15	16
17	18	19	20	21	22	23
24	25	26	27	28	29	30

THURSDAY	FRIDAY	SATURDAY	NOTES
3	4	5	
10	11	12	
17	18	19	
24	25	26	
31			
☐	☐	☐	
☐	☐	☐	
☐	☐	☐	
☐	☐	☐	
☐	☐	☐	

Income and Fixed Expenses

Month: _____   Year: _____

Date	Source of Income	Amount
	Total Income	

Savings	Amount
Total Savings	

Due Date	Fixed Expenses	Amount
	Total Fixed Expenses	

Credit Card	Payment	Balance
	Total	

Total Income		
-	Total Fixed Expenses	
-	Total Credit Card Payment	
-	Total Savings	
Remaining Balance		

Weekly/Monthly Budget

Expense	Budgeted	Actual
Subtotal		

Expense	Budgeted	Actual
Subtotal		

Subtotal		

Subtotal		

Summary	Amount
Previous Balance	
- Total Actual Expenses	
Remaining Balance	

Daily Expenses

Date	Description/Category	Amount
	Total	

Date	Description/Category	Amount
	Total	

Daily Expenses

Date	Description/Category	Amount
	Total	

Date	Description/Category	Amount
	Total	

Ideas and Notes

Ideas and Notes

SEPTEMBER 2023

SUNDAY	MONDAY	TUESDAY	WEDNESDAY
3	4 Labor Day	5	6
10	11	12	13
17	18	19	20
24	25	26	27

AUGUST	SEPTEMBER	OCTOBER

S M T W T F S
       1 2 3 4 5
6 7 8 9 10 11 12
13 14 15 16 17 18 19
20 21 22 23 24 25 26
27 28 29 30 31
	S M T W T F S
	                1 2
	3 4 5 6 7 8 9
	10 11 12 13 14 15 16
	17 18 19 20 21 22 23
	24 25 26 27 28 29 30
		S M T W T F S
		1 2 3 4 5 6 7
		8 9 10 11 12 13 14
		15 16 17 18 19 20 21
		22 23 24 25 26 27 28
		29 30 31

THURSDAY	FRIDAY	SATURDAY	NOTES
	1	2	
7	8	9	
14	15	16	
21	22	23	
28	29	30	
☐	☐	☐	
☐	☐	☐	
☐	☐	☐	
☐	☐	☐	
☐	☐	☐	
THURSDAY	FRIDAY	SATURDAY	NOTES

Income and Fixed Expenses

Month: _____   Year: _____

Date	Source of Income	Amount
	Total Income	

Savings	Amount
Total Savings	

Due Date	Fixed Expenses	Amount
	Total Fixed Expenses	

Credit Card	Payment	Balance
	Total	

Total Income	
- Total Fixed Expenses	
- Total Credit Card Payment	
- Total Savings	
Remaining Balance	

Weekly/Monthly Budget

Expense	Budgeted	Actual
Subtotal		

Expense	Budgeted	Actual
Subtotal		

Expense	Budgeted	Actual
Subtotal		

Expense	Budgeted	Actual
Subtotal		

Summary	Amount
Previous Balance	
- Total Actual Expenses	
Remaining Balance	

Daily Expenses

Date	Description/Category	Amount		Date	Description/Category	Amount
		Total				Total

Daily Expenses

Date	Description/Category	Amount
	Total	

Date	Description/Category	Amount
	Total	

Ideas and Notes

Ideas and Notes

OCTOBER 2023

SUNDAY	MONDAY	TUESDAY	WEDNESDAY
1	2	3	4
8	9 Columbus Day	10	11
15	16	17	18
22	23	24	25
29	30	31	

SEPTEMBER							OCTOBER							NOVEMBER						
S	M	T	W	T	F	S	S	M	T	W	T	F	S	S	M	T	W	T	F	S
					1	2	1	2	3	4	5	6	7				1	2	3	4
3	4	5	6	7	8	9	8	9	10	11	12	13	14	5	6	7	8	9	10	11
10	11	12	13	14	15	16	15	16	17	18	19	20	21	12	13	14	15	16	17	18
17	18	19	20	21	22	23	22	23	24	25	26	27	28	19	20	21	22	23	24	25
24	25	26	27	28	29	30	29	30	31					26	27	28	29	30		

THURSDAY	FRIDAY	SATURDAY	NOTES
5	6	7	
12	13	14	
19	20	21	
26	27	28	
☐	☐	☐	
☐	☐	☐	
☐	☐	☐	
☐	☐	☐	
☐	☐	☐	

Income and Fixed Expenses

Month: _____   Year: _____

Date	Source of Income	Amount
	Total Income	

Savings	Amount
Total Savings	

Due Date	Fixed Expenses	Amount
	Total Fixed Expenses	

Credit Card	Payment	Balance
	Total	

Total Income	
- Total Fixed Expenses	
- Total Credit Card Payment	
- Total Savings	
Remaining Balance	

Weekly/Monthly Budget

Expense	Budgeted	Actual
Subtotal		

Expense	Budgeted	Actual
Subtotal		

Subtotal		

Subtotal		

Summary	Amount
Previous Balance	
- Total Actual Expenses	
Remaining Balance	

Daily Expenses

Date	Description/Category	Amount		Date	Description/Category	Amount
		Total				Total

Daily Expenses

Date	Description/Category	Amount	Date	Description/Category	Amount
		Total			Total

Ideas and Notes

Ideas and Notes

NOVEMBER 2023

SUNDAY	MONDAY	TUESDAY	WEDNESDAY
			1
5	6	7	8
12	13	14	15
19	20	21	22
26	27	28	29

OCTOBER
S	M	T	W	T	F	S
1	2	3	4	5	6	7
8	9	10	11	12	13	14
15	16	17	18	19	20	21
22	23	24	25	26	27	28
29	30	31				

NOVEMBER
S	M	T	W	T	F	S
			1	2	3	4
5	6	7	8	9	10	11
12	13	14	15	16	17	18
19	20	21	22	23	24	25
26	27	28	29	30		

DECEMBER
S	M	T	W	T	F	S
					1	2
3	4	5	6	7	8	9
10	11	12	13	14	15	16
17	18	19	20	21	22	23
24	25	26	27	28	29	30
31						

THURSDAY	FRIDAY	SATURDAY
2	3	4
9	10	11 Veterans Day
16	17	18
23 Thanksgiving Day	24	25
30		

Income and Fixed Expenses

Month: _____   Year: _____

Date	Source of Income	Amount
	Total Income	

Savings	Amount
Total Savings	

Due Date	Fixed Expenses	Amount
	Total Fixed Expenses	

Credit Card	Payment	Balance
	Total	

Total Income	
- Total Fixed Expenses	
- Total Credit Card Payment	
- Total Savings	
Remaining Balance	

Weekly/Monthly Budget

Expense	Budgeted	Actual
Subtotal		

Expense	Budgeted	Actual
Subtotal		

Subtotal		

Subtotal		

Summary	Amount
Previous Balance	
- Total Actual Expenses	
Remaining Balance	

Daily Expenses

Date	Description/Category	Amount
	Total	

Date	Description/Category	Amount
	Total	

Daily Expenses

Date	Description/Category	Amount
	Total	

Date	Description/Category	Amount
	Total	

Ideas and Notes

Ideas and Notes

DECEMBER 2023

SUNDAY	MONDAY	TUESDAY	WEDNESDAY
3	4	5	6
10	11	12	13
17	18	19	20
24	25 Christmas Day	26	27
31			

NOVEMBER
S	M	T	W	T	F	S
			1	2	3	4
5	6	7	8	9	10	11
12	13	14	15	16	17	18
19	20	21	22	23	24	25
26	27	28	29	30		

DECEMBER
S	M	T	W	T	F	S
					1	2
3	4	5	6	7	8	9
10	11	12	13	14	15	16
17	18	19	20	21	22	23
24	25	26	27	28	29	30
31						

JANUARY 2024
S	M	T	W	T	F	S
	1	2	3	4	5	6
7	8	9	10	11	12	13
14	15	16	17	18	19	20
21	22	23	24	25	26	27
28	29	30	31			

THURSDAY	FRIDAY	SATURDAY	NOTES
	1	2	
7	8	9	
14	15	16	
21	22	23	
28	29	30	
☐	☐	☐	
☐	☐	☐	
☐	☐	☐	
☐	☐	☐	
☐	☐	☐	
THURSDAY	FRIDAY	SATURDAY	NOTES

Income and Fixed Expenses

Month: _____   Year: _____

Date	Source of Income	Amount
	Total Income	

Savings	Amount
Total Savings	

Due Date	Fixed Expenses	Amount
	Total Fixed Expenses	

Credit Card	Payment	Balance
	Total	

Total Income	
- Total Fixed Expenses	
- Total Credit Card Payment	
- Total Savings	
Remaining Balance	

Weekly/Monthly Budget

Expense	Budgeted	Actual
Subtotal		

Expense	Budgeted	Actual
Subtotal		

Subtotal		

Subtotal		

Summary	Amount
Previous Balance	
- Total Actual Expenses	
Remaining Balance	

Daily Expenses

Date	Description/Category	Amount
	Total	

Date	Description/Category	Amount
	Total	

Daily Expenses

Date	Description/Category	Amount
	Total	

Date	Description/Category	Amount
	Total	

Ideas and Notes

Savings, Debt, and Bill Trackers

Savings Tracker

Saving for	Amount Needed	Due Date

Date	Deposit	Balance

Saving for	Amount Needed	Due Date

Date	Deposit	Balance

Saving for	Amount Needed	Due Date

Date	Deposit	Balance

Saving for	Amount Needed	Due Date

Date	Deposit	Balance

Savings Tracker

Saving for	Amount Needed	Due Date

Date	Deposit	Balance

Saving for	Amount Needed	Due Date

Date	Deposit	Balance

Saving for	Amount Needed	Due Date

Date	Deposit	Balance

Saving for	Amount Needed	Due Date

Date	Deposit	Balance

Savings Tracker

Saving for	Amount Needed	Due Date

Date	Deposit	Balance

Saving for	Amount Needed	Due Date

Date	Deposit	Balance

Saving for	Amount Needed	Due Date

Date	Deposit	Balance

Saving for	Amount Needed	Due Date

Date	Deposit	Balance

Savings Tracker

Saving for	Amount Needed	Due Date

Date	Deposit	Balance

Saving for	Amount Needed	Due Date

Date	Deposit	Balance

Saving for	Amount Needed	Due Date

Date	Deposit	Balance

Saving for	Amount Needed	Due Date

Date	Deposit	Balance

Debt Tracker

Name of Creditor: _____

Date	Starting Balance	Interest Rate	Minimum Payment	Amount Paid	Ending Balance

Name of Creditor: _____

Date	Starting Balance	Interest Rate	Minimum Payment	Amount Paid	Ending Balance

Debt Tracker

Name of Creditor: _____

Date	Starting Balance	Interest Rate	Minimum Payment	Amount Paid	Ending Balance

Name of Creditor: _____

Date	Starting Balance	Interest Rate	Minimum Payment	Amount Paid	Ending Balance

Debt Tracker

Name of Creditor: _____

Date	Starting Balance	Interest Rate	Minimum Payment	Amount Paid	Ending Balance

Name of Creditor: _____

Date	Starting Balance	Interest Rate	Minimum Payment	Amount Paid	Ending Balance

Debt Tracker

Name of Creditor: _____

Date	Starting Balance	Interest Rate	Minimum Payment	Amount Paid	Ending Balance

Name of Creditor: _____

Date	Starting Balance	Interest Rate	Minimum Payment	Amount Paid	Ending Balance

Debt Tracker

Name of Creditor: _____

Date	Starting Balance	Interest Rate	Minimum Payment	Amount Paid	Ending Balance

Name of Creditor: _____

Date	Starting Balance	Interest Rate	Minimum Payment	Amount Paid	Ending Balance

Debt Tracker

Name of Creditor: _____

Date	Starting Balance	Interest Rate	Minimum Payment	Amount Paid	Ending Balance

Name of Creditor: _____

Date	Starting Balance	Interest Rate	Minimum Payment	Amount Paid	Ending Balance

Debt Tracker

Name of Creditor: _____

Date	Starting Balance	Interest Rate	Minimum Payment	Amount Paid	Ending Balance

Name of Creditor: _____

Date	Starting Balance	Interest Rate	Minimum Payment	Amount Paid	Ending Balance

Debt Tracker

Name of Creditor: _____

Date	Starting Balance	Interest Rate	Minimum Payment	Amount Paid	Ending Balance

Name of Creditor: _____

Date	Starting Balance	Interest Rate	Minimum Payment	Amount Paid	Ending Balance

Holiday Budget

Expense	Budgeted	Actual
Total		

Expense	Budgeted	Actual
Total		

Holiday Gifts

Recipient	Budgeted	Actual
Total		

Recipient	Budgeted	Actual
Total		

Holiday Spending

Date	Description/Category	Amount
	Total	

Date	Description/Category	Amount
	Total	

Bill Tracker

Bill Name	Month					

Bill Tracker

Bill Name \ Month						

Summary for the Year

Month						
Total Income						
Total Expenses						
Balance						
Total Savings						

Monthly Expenses Summary

Category/Expense						

Summary for the Year

Month						
Total Income						
Total Expenses						
Balance						
Total Savings						

Monthly Expenses Summary

Category/Expense						

Accounts Information

Name:	Account:
Website:	Username:
Password/Hint:	
Notes:	

Name:	Account:
Website:	Username:
Password/Hint:	
Notes:	

Name:	Account:
Website:	Username:
Password/Hint:	
Notes:	

Name:	Account:
Website:	Username:
Password/Hint:	
Notes:	

Name:	Account:
Website:	Username:
Password/Hint:	
Notes:	

Name:	Account:
Website:	Username:
Password/Hint:	
Notes:	

Name:	Account:
Website:	Username:
Password/Hint:	
Notes:	

Name:	Account:
Website:	Username:
Password/Hint:	
Notes:	

Accounts Information

Name:	Account:
Website:	Username:
Password/Hint:	
Notes:	

Name:	Account:
Website:	Username:
Password/Hint:	
Notes:	

Name:	Account:
Website:	Username:
Password/Hint:	
Notes:	

Name:	Account:
Website:	Username:
Password/Hint:	
Notes:	

Name:	Account:
Website:	Username:
Password/Hint:	
Notes:	

Name:	Account:
Website:	Username:
Password/Hint:	
Notes:	

Name:	Account:
Website:	Username:
Password/Hint:	
Notes:	

Name:	Account:
Website:	Username:
Password/Hint:	
Notes: